101 PET JOKES

THE HENNESSY KIDS

Art Tutorials by
KHALED ALY

THE HENNESSY ENTERTAINMENT COMPANY

101 Pet Jokes / by The Hennessy Kids

ISBN 978-1-9994854-6-7 (Print)

ISBN 978-1-9994854-7-4 (E-book)

1. Wit and humor, Juvenile. 2. English wit and humor. I. The Hennessy Kids, author

The Hennessy Entertainment Company | HennessyEnt.com |

Copyright © 2022 by The Hennessy Entertainment Company

All rights reserved.

No part of this book may be reproduced in any form or by any electronic or mechanical means, including information storage and retrieval systems, without written permission from the author, except for the use of brief quotations in a book review.

For Dakota, Bubbles, Porsche, Bailey, Jack, Coco, and all the other great pets!

1
LOTS OF PET JOKES

Do bunnies use combs?
    No, they use hare brushes.

Do you want to hear a bad cat joke?
    Just kitten.

How did the bird break into the house?
    With a crow bar.

How do rabbits get from one garden to another?
    They take a taxi cabbage.

How do dog catchers get paid?
    By the pound.

THE HENNESSY KIDS

How do fleas travel from place to place?
    By itch-hiking.

How do you know carrots are good for your eyes?
    Because you never see a rabbit wearing glasses.

How do you stop a dog from barking in your front yard?
    Put him in your backyard.

How does a dog stop a TV show to get a snack?
    She presses the paws button.

How does a mouse feel after it takes a shower?
    Squeaky clean.

How is cat food sold?
    Usually purr can.

How is your cat doing?
    She is feline fine.

How many hairs in a rabbit's tail?
    None - they are all on the outside.

I asked my dog for a joke about the top of our house.
    She said, "Roof roof".

Q:What did the Dalmatian say after his meal?
    "That hit the spots."

There were ten cats in a boat and one jumped out. How many were left?
    None, because they were all copycats.

What airline do rabbits use?
    Hare Canada.

What bird do you always see at lunchtime?
    A swallow.

What kind of dog makes the best watch dog?
    A clocker spaniel.

What did one flea say to the other?
    Should we walk or take a dog?

What did the cowboy say when his puppy was missing?
    "Well, doggone."

What did the dog say to the flea?
>   Quit bugging me.

What did the dog say to the tree?
>   Bark.

What did the dog think when he sat on sandpaper?
>   Rough, rough.

What did the fish say when he got out of jail?
>   "I'm off the hook."

What did the rabbit give his girlfriend?
>   A 14 carrot ring.

What do bunnies sing at birthday parties?
>   Hoppy birthday to you.

What do cats like to eat on sunny days?
>   Mice cream cones.

Where do cats like to look at for shopping ideas?
>   Cat-alogues.

What do cats wear at night?
> Paw-jamas.

What do fish need to stay healthy?
> Vitamin sea.

What do you call a bunny that has fleas?
> Bugs Bunny.

What do you call a bunny transformer?
> Hop-timus Prime.

What do you call a cat on ice?
> One cool cat.

What do you call a cat that can handle a catastrophe?
> A survival kit.

What do you call a cat that does tricks?
> A magic kit.

What do you call a cat that gets anything it wants?
> Purrr-suasive.

What's the secret to good-smelling cats?
　Prrrr-fume.

What do you call a dog magician?
　A labracadabrador.

What do you call a dog with a Timex?
　A watch dog.

What do you call a frozen dog?
　A pupsicle.

What do you call a great dog detective?
　Sherlock Bones.

What do you call a kitten that likes to cuddle?
　Paws-tively purrrfect.

What do you call a large dog that pays attention to her surroundings?
　Aware wolf.

What do you call a newbie hamster?
　Hamateur.

What is the rudest bird in the world?
  A mockingbird.

What do you call an operation on a rabbit?
  A hare-cut.

What do you call it when a cat wins a dog show?
  A cat-has-trophy.

What do you do if you catch your dog eating your dictionary?
  You take the words right out of his mouth.

What do you get if you cross a gold dog with a telephone?
  A golden receiver.

What do you get when you cross a frog and a dog?
  A croaker spaniel.

What do you get when you cross a parrot and a centipede?
  A walkie-talkie.

What do you get when you cross a rabbit with a leaf blower?
  A hare dryer.

What do you get when you pour hot water into a cranky rabbit's home?
A hot cross bunny.

What do you give a dog who behaves really well?
A bone-us.

What do you give a sick bird?
Tweetment.

What does a bird like in his soup?
Crowtons.

What does my dog and my phone have in common?
They both have collar I.D.

What dog can jump higher than a tree?
Any dog can jump higher than a tree, trees can't jump.

What happened when a hundred hares escaped from the school's rabbit farm?
The teachers had to comb the area.

What happened when the dog went to the flea circus?
He stole the show.

What has fur and whiskers and cuts grass?
A lawn meower.

What is a dog's favourite food?
Anything that is on your plate.

What is a mouse's favourite game?
Hide and squeak.

What is small, squeaky, and great at sword fights?
A mouseketeer.

What kind of cats like to go bowling?
Alley cats.

What kind of dog does Dracula have?
A bloodhound.

What kind of dog keeps the best time?
A watch dog.

What kind of pet is the least expensive?
The budgie - it's cheep cheep.

THE HENNESSY KIDS

What month do dogs bark the least?
    February - it is the shortest month.

What side of a cat has more fur?
    The outside.

What type of market should you never take your dog?
    A flea market.

What's a dog's favourite kind of pizza?
    Pupperoni pizza.

What's a dog's ideal research job?
    Barkeologist.

What's grey, squeaky and hangs around in caves?
    Stalagmice.

Whats the best way to catch a fish?
    Have someone throw it to you gently.

Where does a hamster go for Spring Break?
    Hamsterdam.

Which breed of dog is the quietest?
    A hush puppy.

Which dog breed is guaranteed to laugh at all of your jokes?
    A Chi-ha-ha.

Who do fish always know how much they weigh?
    Because they have their own scales.

Why are cats so good at video games?
    Because they have nine lives.

Why aren't dogs good dancers?
    Because they have two left feet.

Why did the cat cross the road?
    It was the chicken's day off.

Why did the cat put the letter "M" into the fridge?
    Because it turns "ice" into "mice".

Why did the Dalmatian go to the eye doctor?
    He kept seeing spots.

Why did the dog cross the road twice?
    He was trying to fetch a boomerang.

Why do dogs wag their tails?
    Because no one else will do it for them.

Why is a tree like a noisy dog?
    They both have a lot of bark.

Why is it against the law to let an eagle get sick?
    Because then it is illegal.

Why was the mouse afraid of the water?
    He saw a catfish.

Why did the doctor have a Labrador retriever and kitten at work?
    In case she needed to do a cat scan or get a lab report.

2

KNOCK-KNOCK JOKES

Knock, knock.
   Who's there?
   Champ.
   Champ who?
   Champoo the dog, he was sprayed by a skunk!

Knock, knock.
   Who's there?
   Dude.
   Dude who?
   Dude-doo in the yard, need to scoop it up.

3
ARTWORK

THE HENNESSY KIDS

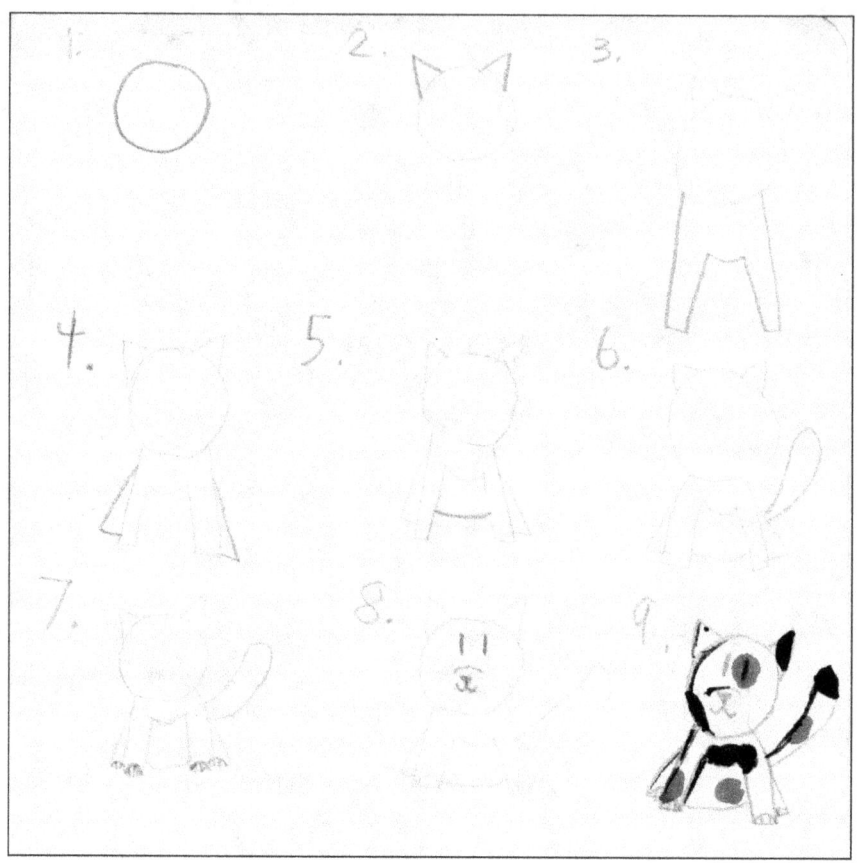

"How To Draw A Cat" by Khaled Aly

101 PET JOKES

"How To Draw A Dog" by Khaled Aly

4

A FEW MORE PET JOKES

What's the difference between a strange rabbit and a strong rabbit?
One is a bit funny, and the other is a fit bunny.

Did you ever see a fish bowl?
Yes.
Did she get a strike or a spare?

How did the Scottish dog feel when he saw the Loch Ness monster?
Terrier-fied.

The more the rabbit takes away from it, the bigger it becomes. What is it?
A rabbit hole.

"All hundred sheep are in now," the talking sheepdog told the farmer.

"But I only have ninety-five sheep," says the farmer.

"I know," replies the sheepdog. "But I rounded them up."

My friend and I both have cats. My cat's name is One Two Three, and her cat's name is Un Deux Trois.

Our cats raced across the pond - guess who won?

One Two Three won, because Un Deux Trois cat sank.

5

SUBMITTED JOKE

Here's a joke sent to us from Lil Mac.

Where do cats go to recycle?
    The litter box.

6

YOUR FAVOURITE JOKE

What is your favourite pet joke that isn't in this book?

Send it to us at thehennessykids@gmail.com, and we'll look to share it online with all our friends!

ACKNOWLEDGMENTS

Special thank you to Khaled Aly for sharing how to draw cats and dogs.

Thank you for reading our book! We hope you enjoyed it. Please tell these jokes to your friends and family and make more people happy.

ACKNOWLEDGMENTS

The Hennessy Kids think the world would be better with more smiles.

Want to know when our new books are available? Sign up for our **Fun Stuff With Heart** newsletter at HennessyEnt.com!

BOOKS BY THE HENNESSY KIDS

101 Halloween Jokes

101 Christmas Jokes

101 Pet Jokes

101 Knock Knock Jokes, Vol. 1

101 Nature Jokes

101 Food Jokes

www.ingramcontent.com/pod-product-compliance
Lightning Source LLC
Chambersburg PA
CBHW052127070526
44586CB00016B/2119